BUDDHIST
WISDOM

DAVID CROSWELLER

BUDDHIST WISDOM

DAILY REFLECTIONS

TUTTLE PUBLISHING
Tokyo • Rutland, Vermont • Singapore

To Amy, Kathryn, Ellie, Murphy and Carina

This edition first published in the United States in 2003 by Tuttle Publishing, an imprint of Periplus Editions (HK) Ltd., with editorial offices at 364 Innovation Drive, North Clarendon, Vermont 05759.

The extracts in this book were previously published in the United States in 1999 as *Reflections of Buddha for Every Day*.

Library of Congress Control Number: 2002116403
ISBN-10: 0-8048-3489-X
ISBN-13: 978-0-8048-3489-6

First edition
10 09 08 07   10 9 8 7 6 5 4 3

Edited and designed by
Eddison Sadd Editions Limited
St Chad's House
148 King's Cross Road
London WC1X 9DH

Distributed by:
Tuttle Publishing, 364 Innovation Drive,
North Clarendon, VT 05759.
Tel: (802)773-8930; Fax:(802)773-6993
E-mail: info@tuttlepublishing.com
www.tuttlepublishing.com

Phototypeset in Berkley Old Style BT and Gill Sans using QuarkXPress on Apple Macintosh
Printed in Singapore

TUTTLE PUBLISHING® is a registered trademark of Tuttle Publishing, a division of Periplus Editions (HK) Ltd.

Contents

Introduction

Buddhism is a tradition that offers all individuals, regardless of religious persuasion, a way of exploring the true role and purpose of our lives as human beings. The tradition takes its name from the word 'Buddha', which means 'the awakened one'. Put simply, the goal of Buddhists is to awaken to the true nature of reality. This is not just an intellectual process: rather, it is one which engages the whole person and typically involves the awakening of the heart just as much as the mind.

There is a particular story that is familiar in Buddhist teachings. In this story, four men (sometimes it is said they are blind) are asked to feel a strange animal in the darkness and identify it. The first man feels its head, the second its ear, the third its tusk and the fourth its tail, and each exclaims they know what it is, pronouncing 'it' to be a pot, a win-nowing fan, a plough and a broom respectively. The Buddha used this story to illustrate the life we all endure and the views held by some of his more animated followers. He said:

> *'Those people, blind unseeing, without knowing the truth,*
> *each maintain that it is like this and like that'*

Although many volumes of literature have accumulated over the centuries based on the teachings of the Buddha, Buddhism is essentially a non dogmatic religion. The Buddha himself wrote down not a word, and the first validated texts were recorded some four hundred years after his death. Although a number of different interpretations of his teachings have evolved over the centuries, there are certain principles to which all Buddhist schools subscribe. However, none of them prescribe a specific set of beliefs: rather, they stress the fundamental importance of direct religious experience.

Many Buddhist practices offer ways of exploring and responding to the kind of questions that have preoccupied people for centuries: 'Who am I?', 'Why am I here?' and 'What is life and what does it mean?' The basis of Buddhist teaching is not about what to believe; it is about what we can do to deepen our understanding of ourselves, and in so doing learn how to penetrate the mystery at the heart of life.

BUDDHISM TODAY
During the course of the twentieth century, Buddhism has declined drastically in Asia, partly due to the materialistic

emphasis of modern consumer culture, and partly because of the devastating impact of successive Communist revolutions whose leaders have done their best to eradicate all kinds of religious practice. However, at the same time, Buddhist teachings have started to flourish in the West. Today, there are Buddhist centres across Europe, North America and Australia, with the number of converts growing every year. In fact, it is believed there are now more Buddhists than ever before.

HOW TO USE THIS BOOK

In the same way you have been drawn to these reflections, I was drawn to the reflections of my own teacher. He inspired me to bring the teachings of the Buddha to a wider audience through the same medium. The first offering was as individual cards, each carrying a saying of the Buddha, together with an altar, booklet and mandala. This second offering allows a more compact view of the same inspiring reflections.

I have drawn the reflections from a number of sources, chiefly 'The Dhammapada', widely regarded as the most accurate of the recorded versions of the Buddha's teaching. The remainder of the reflections are from a variety of established texts – each of which is referenced – attributed to the Buddha. I studied numerous versions of all the texts referenced, including 'raw text' translations, and came up with my own interpretations. I hope the translation and the random order in which the reflections have been presented meet with your approval.

You may, as a matter of routine, choose to open the book at today's date and meditate on the reflection as shown.

Perhaps you could carry the book with you during the day or make a note of today's reflection and refer to it when you have a quiet moment. Alternatively, you may just like to open the book at random. You may have a question or an issue uppermost in your mind and whichever option you choose, the reflection may give you an insight as to where you might find the answer. The reflection may be one you like, or maybe it makes you feel uncomfortable. Whatever your first response, give yourself time to absorb it, and take it with you into the activities of the day. You may find that its significance reveals itself at an unexpected moment, or comes back to you when it is the furthest thing from your thoughts.

One thing is good to remember – the Buddha taught that there are no rules. Everything is completely up to you.

You are fortunate to be born a human being,
but it is difficult to live life properly,
even harder to follow a spiritual path
and most difficult to attain Nirvana.

The Buddha, verse 182

A single step on the path of enlightenment is greater than being ruler of the universe.

The World, verse 178

If you don't have a settled mind and
don't understand the scriptures, there is little
hope for you. However, if you have a mind
steady in thoughts of purity, and unaffected
by good or bad, then you will be aware
of your destiny, free from fear.

Thoughts, verses 38 & 39

The Eternal is found!
You can learn the doctrine
and if you follow what you
are taught then you will
attain that which many seek.

Buddhacarita

A wise person does not damage his or her environment.

Flowers, verse 49

Who ranks as the Highest?
One who *owns* nothing,
desires nothing,
is *attached* to nothing.

The Highest, verse 421

Live your life in happiness,
even though those around you
live their lives in hatred and wish
to spread their antipathy to you.
Be happiness itself.

Happiness, verse 197

It is better to die in battle against temptation than to live as its slave.

Padhama Sutta

A true holy person accepts
what he or she is given,
and is never envious.
Envy does not assist meditation.

The Holy Person, verse 365

Nothing holds tighter than attachment to family and money. Break these attachments by overcoming desire, and turn your back on material and sensual pleasures.

Desires, verses 345 & 346

The eightfold path is the sure way of cleansing one's mind, overcoming temptation and ending suffering.

The Right Way, verses 274 & 275

If you are virtuous and follow a proper life,
there will be no wanting in your life.
This is in accord with nature.

Anguttara Nikaya

Ford the fiercest stream of life and
overcome desire.
Go beyond delusion and opposites.
Concentrate on your practice.
Attachment will fall away from you
and you will know truth.

The Highest, verses 383 & 384

Goodwill towards all
is true religion.

Buddhacarita

All beings wish for happiness,
so extend your compassion
to everyone.

Mahavamsa

Enjoy only the company
of the good, not the bad.

The Wise Person, verse 78

Even those who have taken holy
orders can be bad and ill-disciplined
and they will go to hell.
It is better to swallow a red-hot ball
of iron than to live falsely on the
generosity of others.

Hell, verses 307 & 308

Live in accord with nature,
and if you are joyous there
will be no wanting in your life.
This will give you great relaxation.

Anguttara Nikaya

If you can still your mind,
still as a broken gong,
you will leave all unrest behind
and attain Nirvana.

Retribution, verse 134

Craving brings only sadness and fear. Avoid craving and you avoid sadness and fear.

Pleasure, verse 216

One hundred years without seeing either the deathless state or the Absolute Truth is nothing compared to the joy of a single day of true vision.

The Thousands, verses 114 & 115

It is only you who can master your self.
But once this is done, it is a rare blessing.

Self, verse 160

The road is long for the weary as is the night for those who cannot sleep. Longer still is the cycle of birth and death for those not following a spiritual path.

The Novice, verse 60

You are criticized if you talk too *much*.
You are criticized if you talk too *little*.
You are criticized if you talk just *enough*.
No one escapes criticism.

Anger, verse 227

A real gift is one for which
nothing is required in return.

Prasnottaramalika

If you are without fear and desire,
have no attachments and understand
the scriptures for what they really say,
then this birth is your last.

Desires, verses 351 & 352

Having gone through many cycles of birth and death, the time will come when you are aware of the orchestrator of the merry-go-round. When this happens you need not be tempted at the fairground again, but walk straight through on the way to Nirvana.

Old Age, verses 153 & 154

If you do something bad,
don't enjoy it, or repeat it,
or allow it to become a
way of life.

Bad Conduct, verse 117

Don't try to do too much, too quickly.
Cleanse your mind of flaws little by little,
making sure the job is well done.
For if this is not done properly, then bad
deeds will consume those who action them.

Flaws, verses 239 & 240

Don't seek happiness
through the pain of others,
for this is a trap from which
you cannot escape.

Other Things, verse 291

It is good to be a loving child to your parents.
It is good to be a renunciant.
It is good to be virtuous in old age.
It is good to be held in high esteem.
But to achieve lasting joy,
it is good to become enlightened.

The Elephant, verses 332 & 333

If you are maligned by the world,
do not harbor bad thoughts against it.

Sammaparibbajaniya Sutta

Be wise.
Learn what is real and what is not,
what is necessary and what is not.
Set your sights high and work
steadfastly towards your goal.

The Opposites, verses 11 & 12

Be fixed on your actions,
be they great or small.
Lead a blameless life and
speak kindly to all.

Mahaparinibbana Sutta

Effort given to satisfying bodily desires is rewarded only with sadness and fear. Avoid bodily desires and you avoid sadness and fear.

Pleasure, verse 215

Who ranks as the Highest?
One who acts properly. A recluse
who has a pure mind and a
traveller who has renounced all.
One who is never angry and who
never responds to others' anger.

The Highest, verses 388 & 389

If you do something good,
enjoy it, repeat it, allow it to
become a way of life.

Bad Conduct, verse 118

Adultery will only lead to loss of status, lack of sleep, disgrace and an increase in suffering.

What joy can there be when both parties are frightened of the consequences?

Don't do it.

Hell, verses 309 & 310

If you help others purely for
the sake of helping, with no
thought of personal gain and
without wishing to be recognized
for the help you give, you can
be called truly virtuous.

Jatakamala

Don't fall into temptation,
don't desire material things.
Meditate and achieve the greatest joy.

Awareness, verse 27

Keep your mind fixed on
The Buddha and be steady in your
practice both day and night.

Other Things, verses 296 & 297

You have to know how to follow your own practice, before the time arrives when you can help others to follow theirs. This is not an easy task to master.

Self, verse 159

Who ranks as the Highest?
One who is not afraid of breaking
attachment, who has cast out anger
and desire, and lifted the barrier which
prevented any forward movement.

The Highest, verses 397 & 398

If you train and direct your mind along paths you want it to travel, you will achieve great happiness.

Thoughts, verses 35 & 36

If a person is still full of greed and desire, how can the shaving of their head make them virtuous?
The true initiate has no desire and no greed.

A Proper Life, verses 264 & 265

Meditate. Now meditate some more.
Do not crave material pleasures and then cry
for your loss. Only the wise can gain wisdom
from meditation, and this is not for all.
Fixed in meditation you will find Nirvana.

The Holy Person, verses 371 & 372

As night follows day,

so life reaches its end.

A human's life simply stops.

Samyutta Nikaya

There is nothing sweeter
than practice of truth.
It has the sweetest taste
and gives the greatest joy.
It will end suffering.

Desires, verse 354

If you are absorbed in acquiring family,
money and possessions, death will
come and sweep you away.
No one can save you from this.
So seize the time, learn your practice
and follow the path that leads to Nirvana.

The Right Way, verses 287, 288 & 289

If you don't take care of each other
who will take care of you?
Look after the sick as you would
look after yourself.

Buddhacarita

The novice may seek glory and power
from his or her fellow aspirants.
This is wrong, as it will only
increase their conceit.

The Novice, verses 73 & 74

Strife can only cause more strife.
Only an open heart can put an end to strife.
This is a Universal Law.
Remember the center point during a
disagreement and strife will quickly end.

The Opposites, verses 5 & 6

Trained elephants used to
carry kings into battle.
Train your mind to carry
the weight of criticism.

The Elephant, verse 321

There is no *fire* like passion.
There is no *grasp* like hate.
There is no *trap* like illusion.
There is no *flood* like craving.

Flaws, verse 251

Enjoy the beauty of your practice.
In the depths of your meditation
experience the nectar of spiritual joy.

Happiness, verse 205

Give freely to others
and live a proper life.
Act in a way that will give
no one the chance to criticize.
This is a true blessing.

Mahamangala Sutta

Wherever an enlightened being lives,
be it in a village or a forest,
on a mountain or in a valley,
it will be known as a holy place and,
regardless of the environment, he or she
will be at peace, and experience only joy.

The Enlightened One, verses 98 & 99

Meditation leads you to wisdom.
No meditation leaves you where
you are. Make up your mind
where you would rather be.

20. The Right Way, verse 282

By what path will you reach
the Buddha, who is free from
all desire, all attachment and
all social conditioning?

The Buddha, verse 180

Give up the dark side and be in the light.

Seek happiness in solitude and not in material pleasures.

Leave everything behind and regard nothing as your own.

Follow your practice.

Having done this, enlightenment will follow.

The Wise Person, verses 87, 88 & 89

Live in accord with nature
and be free from regret,
and great satisfaction will
be your reward.

Anguttara Nikaya

You have to do the work,
no one else can do it for you.
Follow the eightfold path and
continue your practice,
and you will soar beyond
the clutches of temptation.

The Right Way, verse 276

Who ranks as the Highest?
One who is settled in meditation.
One who has reached the other side.
One who is at peace.

The Highest, verse 414

Bad actions will always cause great suffering to those who create them.

Self, verse 162

In the noble eightfold path,
what is Right Concentration?
To be free of desire and not to allow
the torment of the mind to have any effect.
To be in that secluded place where there
is true awareness of joy and happiness.
This is the first level of concentration.

Digha Nikaya

Remember the body is not real.
If you focus on this you will
overcome temptations and break
this cycle of birth and death.

Flowers, verse 46

Does your mind wander when it wants to?
Exercise discipline and control it,
as a mahout controls the elephant.

The Elephant, verse 326

There are those who are afraid
for the wrong reason and not afraid
for the wrong reason.
These people are on the wrong path.

Hell, verse 317

Don't live a bad life,
be cautious in what you believe
and think of others at all times.
Don't be trapped in the world.

The World, verse 167

Who ranks as the Highest?
One who has no desire at all,
not even for enlightenment.
One who has no attachments.
One who is free from doubt.
One who has gone beyond that
which you can understand.

The Highest, verses 410 & 411

Regardless of your birth or your upbringing, seek the pure incomparable peace that is Nirvana.
Once attained, rest in the knowledge that there is no coming back.

Majjhima Nikaya

Who will enjoy looking at you when there is no flesh on your bones?

Old Age, verse 149

If you do bad things you will feel fine
until eventually you reap the consequences.
Then you will know only suffering.

Bad Conduct, verse 119

Through awareness and perseverance you can break this cycle of birth and death and find yourself elevated to the highest. Therefore, awareness leads you forward, while lack of awareness leads you nowhere.

Awareness, verse 21

There is no happiness
except that found in right action.

Attanagaluvimsa

Don't see others' faults,
see your own.
For if you dwell on others' faults,
your own get stronger.

Flaws, verses 252 & 253

It doesn't matter if you look like a renunciant;
if you don't follow your practice, you are a sham.
If you follow your practice sincerely, you can
dress however you wish for all it matters.
It's the practice that counts.

Retribution, verses 141 & 142

A Buddha is not easy to find,
for one is not born just anywhere.
However, where one is found
you will also find great happiness.

The Buddha, verse 193

Riches harm all, except those who undertake steady practice. Greedy people harm themselves and others.

Desires, verse 355

If you can look at situations with
a balanced point of view, without
attachment or indulging in harmful acts,
then it may be said that you are living
a proper life, a righteous life.

A Proper Life, verses 256 & 257

Be your own worst critic, but also recognize your successes. Protect yourself and train yourself, and in this way you will live in great happiness.

The Holy Person, verses 379 & 380

If you have faith and live a proper life,
then people will be drawn to you.
For those who are good shine like a
mountain peak, while those who are
bad disappear into the darkest valley.

Other Things, verses 303 & 304

In the noble eightfold path,
what is Right Livelihood?
Right Livelihood is not deceiving others
and not seeking personal gain.

Digha Nikaya

Don't dwell upon the faults of others, dwell upon your own.

Flowers, verse 50

Be wise, disciplined and non-violent
and you will find peace.
Be aware both night and day,
continue your practice,
and you will attain Nirvana.

Anger, verses 225 & 226

Emotional ties bring only sadness and fear.
Avoid attachment in emotion and
you avoid sadness and fear.

Pleasure, verse 213

Turn your mind away from things
which are not permanent.

Majjhima Nikaya

Who ranks as the Highest?
One who is knowledgeable and wise.
One who follows the correct path.
One who is not attached to anything.
One who needs nothing.

The Highest, verses 403 & 404

Not everyone who wears a
holy robe is worthy to do so.
Without purifying the mind first
they are indulging in self-deception.
Those who have found the center point
are worthy of your consideration.

The Opposites, verses 9 & 10

If a person believes that
'these children, this wealth, is mine',
then they are not a worthy companion.

The Novice, verse 62

Whether the world is eternal or not,
whether it is infinite or not,
one thing is certain: there will be
birth, old age, death and suffering.

Buddhacarita

A true holy person delights in what he or she
is given, regardless of how much or how little.
They are not attached to anything and
live a life of loving kindness towards all.
Such a life will find that place of peace.

The Holy Person, verses 366, 367 & 368

Those with a closed heart
will go nowhere.
Those with an open heart in all
things will find great happiness.

The World, verse 177

Delusion corrupts, as weeds choke a field. Be free of delusion, and honor those who are also free.

Desires, verse 358

Be wary of negativity.
Get yourself out of the darkness
which waits to trap you.

The Elephant, verse 327

Be conscious of how you live your life.
Meditate, help others, maintain a
pure mind and be alert to your
discipline, and others will
become aware of your efforts.

Awareness, verse 24

Do not believe in something solely
because someone has told you so,
or tradition has it, or because many others do.
Test for yourself, experience for yourself.

Kalama Sutta

Who ranks as the Highest?
One who is a wanderer
without passion.

The Highest, verse 415

The *mantra* is of no use when not chanted.
The *house* decays when it is not repaired.
The *body* deteriorates when it is not cared for.
The *guard* fails when the eyes close.

Flaws, verse 241

Suffering arrives in ten ways if you
harm the innocent: pain, calamity,
accident, illness, insanity, legal problems,
accusations, death or financial ruin;
or your house may be burnt down.
Following this you will go to hell.

Retribution, verses 137, 138, 139 & 140

Support your parents, and
care for your own family.
Follow peace at all times.
This is a true blessing.

Mahamangala Sutta

Would you rather have a trivial pleasure
or the greatest happiness?
Make sacrifices to attain the latter.

Other Things, verse 290

Live one meditative day well, with
morality, wisdom and goodness,
rather than a hundred years badly.

The Thousands, verses 110 & 111

Be your own light. Be your own refuge.
Confide in nothing outside of yourself.
Hold fast to Truth that it may be your guide.
Hold fast to Truth that it may be your protector.

Mahaparinibbana Sutta

Material gain or Nirvana?
As an aspirant, a disciple of Buddha,
you should ignore the former
and strive for the latter.

The Novice, verse 75

You will suffer in this life and the next
both from the actions and the
knowledge of things you do wrong.
If you do good, you can achieve
overwhelming happiness in this world
which will also be with you in the next.

The Opposites, verses 17 & 18

Words may be beautiful, but like
the unscented flower, they do not
necessarily carry sincerity,
whereas the scented flower delivers
what its beauty decrees. Your words
should carry conviction in the same way.

Flowers, verses 51 & 52

Avoid all bad things,
only do good things
and cleanse your mind.
This is the teaching
of the Buddha.

The Buddha, verse 183

No matter how hard you may strive
to reach the other shore, few succeed.
However, persevere, and you will get there
in the end, beyond the reach of death.

The Wise Person, verses 85 & 86

I take my refuge in the *Buddha*.
I take my refuge in the *Dhamma*.
I take my refuge in the *Sangha*.

The slightest trace of desire will keep
you suckling on the teat of materialism.
Remove every desire, as you would
pluck an autumn lotus.
Follow the Buddha's path to Nirvana.

The Right Way, verses 284 & 285

Triumph creates enmity, and
those defeated live in pain.
Be neither the victor
nor the vanquished,
but live at peace with all.

Happiness, verse 201

Do your duty,
show kindness to others
and keep them from suffering.

Avadana Sutta

Like fresh milk, it takes time
for a bad deed to turn sour.
Like a smoldering fire,
it burns the novice slowly.

The Novice, verse 71

You could be born again or,
if you do bad deeds, enter a world of suffering,
and if you do good deeds, enter a world of joy.
However, those who have found enlightenment
attain Nirvana.

Bad Conduct, verse 126

A person not following a spiritual path grows large around the waist, but not large in knowledge.

Old Age, verse 152

Always be aware.
Constantly devote yourself to
the cleansing of your own mind.
In this way you will be your own
salvation.

Mahaparinibbana sutta

If a person ignores the spiritual path and believes life is simply for satisfying desires, then on the day they see an aspirant engaged in practice, living a life of peace, they will feel pangs of envy.

Pleasure, verse 209

Once you control your thoughts, which will wander all over the place if given the chance, you will escape the clutches of temptation.

Thoughts, verse 37

It is not certain that ritual, study,
meditation, mindfulness or a
solitary life will bring you Nirvana.
But you can achieve this,
simply by living a proper life.

A Proper Life, verses 271 & 272

Who ranks as the Highest?
One who follows the teachings of the Buddha.

The Highest, verse 392

In the noble eightfold path,
what is Right Mindfulness?
Whatever one is doing, whether
sitting, reclining, walking or running,
inwardly be aware of the physical body.
Recognize that you are not the body,
and you will be free of everything.

Digha Nikaya

Once your longing for knowledge
has been awakened, and the
temptations of the world overcome,
you are certain to ford the stream of life.

Pleasure, verse 218

Neither money nor sensual
pleasures will satisfy your desires.
Worldly things only cause more suffering,
and a true follower of the Buddha
dispenses with them.

The Buddha, verses 186 & 187

All craftspeople ply their trade,
and spiritual aspirants are no different.
They have trained their minds,
not their hands.

The Wise Person, verse 80

Destroy desire and conceit, lust and ego.
This is the way the true spiritual seeker
is freed from the cycle of birth and death.

Other Things, verses 294 & 295

Passion corrupts, as weeds choke a field. Be free of passion, and honor those who are also free.

Desires, verse 356

Think clearly and learn well.
Have control over yourself
and speak kindly to all.
This is a true blessing.

Mahamangala Sutta

Enjoy the gifts of others,
be you the receiver or not.
Each person gives for their own reason,
and to worry about why will
destroy your peace of mind.

Flaws, verses 249 & 250

Who ranks as the Highest?
One who has no thought of good and bad.
One who is free from suffering,
desire and impurity.

The Highest, verse 412

Persevere with your
meditation and you
will attain the
greatest freedom,
Nirvana.

Awareness, verse 23

You can perform a thousand rituals
for a hundred years, or tend a sacrificial
fire in a forest for a thousand years,
but to pay homage to an enlightened being
will bring you much greater reward.

The Thousands, verses 106 & 107

Control your eyes, ears, nose,
body, mind and thought.
With such control, a holy person
will be free from suffering.

The Holy Person, verses 360 & 361

All fear retribution.
All fear death. All love life.
Do not kill or cause others to kill.

Retribution, verses 129 & 130

If you are in a position
of power over others,
be very gentle with them.

Udanavarga

Bad actions create bad consequences.
Good actions create good consequences.
Undertake only good actions, but make
sure you protect yourself and don't waste
even a second. For time wasted means you
are not going forwards quickly enough.

Hell, verses 314 & 315

To wish for a little summer house
here, a little winter house there,
and another somewhere else,
is not the way to remain focused
on your true goal, Nirvana.

The Right Way, verse 286

It is better to spend time with
the wise and enlightened,
rather than fools.

Happiness, verse 206

You can suffer in this world and the next,
or you can live your life properly.
Rejoice in the happiness of now,
safe in the knowledge of the future.

The Opposites, verses 15 & 16

Don't give in to anger
under any circumstances.

Anger, verse 222

The sun shines by day and the moon by night. What the warrior achieves in battle, so the Highest achieves in meditation. Whatever the time, the Buddha forever shines in love for all.

The Highest, verse 387

Ambition and anger will disappear
when you stop concerning yourself
with the fruits of your actions.

lalita Vistara

Think well of yourself,
but always be cautious.

Self, verse 157

Carry out your good deeds with a stout heart and you shall be happy, content and without suffering.

The Novice, verse 68

If you hurt an innocent person,
then you are only hurting yourself,
just as dust thrown into a wind
is blown back in your face.

Bad Conduct, verse 125

Do not indulge in charitable acts
for your own benefit. Love them
for the happiness they bring to others.

Jatakamala

Who ranks as the Highest?
One who does not harm anything.
One who never retaliates.
One who is always at peace regardless
of the other person's disposition.

The Highest, verses 405 & 406

The Buddha is victory
beyond all victories.
By what path will you
reach the Buddha?

The Buddha, verse 179

Constant talk does not mean wisdom.
On the other hand, the signs of patience,
love and freedom will direct you
towards the wise person.

A Proper Life, verse 258

Be like the Buddha.
Conquer yourself and live a proper life.
Have nothing and live in freedom.
Once you have done this,
where will you find a teacher?

Desires, verse 353

Trained mules, horses and elephants are all useful, but a well-trained mind is even more so. No trained animal can lead you to Nirvana, but a well-trained mind can.

The Elephant, verses 322 & 323

Without a staff or a sword,
the Buddhist is kind and sympathetic,
and gives love and compassion towards
all living beings.

Majjhima Nikaya

It is easy to be bad,
more difficult to be good.

Self, verse 163

Live your life in happiness,
even though those around you
live their lives in hatred and wish
to spread their antipathy to you.
Be happiness itself.

Happiness, verse 197

If you make vows, stick to them.
If it is worth doing, do it properly.
A half-hearted renunciant
does more harm than good.

Hell, verses 312 & 313

It is the nature of things
that doubt shall arise.

Buddhacarita

As a farmer irrigates the fields,
as an archer guides the arrow,
and as a carpenter shapes the wood,
so the true disciple molds his or
her mind.

Retribution, verse 145

We are used to discussing duality,
existence and non-existence,
but if you understand,
with truth and wisdom,
how things begin and end,
for you there will be no existence
and non-existence.

Samyutta Nikaya

An untrained mind cannot resist
the torrent of desire, while one that
is steeped in practice and discipline
is able to deflect any temptations,
like a house with a solid roof remaining
watertight in a shower of rain.

The Opposites, verses 13 & 14

Once one bad thought,
word or deed has been
created by someone,
they are capable of much worse.

The World, verse 176

Even when the novice learns
a little, it tends to be misused,
and eventually causes him or her
a serious headache.

The Novice, verse 72

Who ranks as the Highest?
One who speaks gently and truthfully.
One who asks for nothing and gives everything.

The Highest, verses 408 & 409

Desire leads to rebirth.
This is accompanied by pleasure,
and finding satisfaction in one thing
and then another leads to a desire
for rebirth and the desire for death.

Digha Nikaya

The true holy person who follows their
practice and the words of the Buddha,
who applies that teaching to their everyday life,
will light up the world with their beauty.

The Holy Person, verses 381 & 382

Avoid doing physical harm, causing
mental anguish or using harsh words.
Use body, mind and speech only for good,
for such is the way of an enlightened being.

Anger, verses 231, 232, 233 & 234

Your skeletal frame is like the foundation of a house, and flesh and blood the plaster. Old age and death, pride and deception live in the house.

Old Age, verse 150

The fragrance of flowers cannot be smelled if you stand downwind, but the fragrance of good actions can be recognized anywhere.

Flowers, verse 54

An elephant in a rut will
not eat and is hard to control.

The Elephant, verse 324

You can be blessed with faith,
virtue, knowledge, charity and wisdom,
but a single desire will lead you to rebirth.

Majjhima Nikaya

Use wisdom, be free from
attachment and defeat temptation,
not just for now, but forever.
For your body will soon give up its
worth to you, once life has left it.

Thoughts, verses 40 & 41

In the noble eightfold path,
what is Right Effort?
Right Effort is that which will create
the necessary conditions for the mind
to be focused, allowing clarity and
concentration in order that you may
achieve completion in your task.

Digha Nikaya

Desires will trap you like a spider
caught in its own web.
Break free of desires and
break free of suffering.

Desires, verse 347

Live in accord with nature,
and when you can concentrate properly
there will be no wanting in your life.
This will enable you to see things as they are.

Anguttara Nikaya

Make every effort not to indulge in negative thoughts, cruel words and bad deeds.

The Right Way, verse 281

Who ranks as the Highest?
One who endures all hardships equally.
One who is patient and strong.
One who never gives in to anger.
One who is experiencing their final body.

The Highest, verses 399 & 400

Once you are able to control your senses
and are free from pride – patient and
steadfast – even the gods will cast
envious looks at you.
You will be like a crystal-clear lake
and have no need to consider rebirth.

The Enlightened One, verses 94 & 95

Neither pretty words nor a pretty face
can make an envious, deceitful and
greedy person beautiful of heart.
Only those without these traits
can be known as such.

A Proper Life, verses 262 & 263

Don't allow yourself to become free from one kind of suffering, only to be caught in another.

Desires, verse 344

If you, the spiritual seeker,
are forever aware, you will advance
quickly towards your goal.
With this attitude you will not be deterred;
in fact, you will have almost attained Nirvana.

Awareness, verses 31 & 32

Do good deeds, not bad.
If you do not undertake good deeds,
bad deeds become a way of life.

Bad Conduct, verse 116

Those who break society's rules and who
also drink too much are killing themselves.
They have no discipline.
Be aware of this and don't let
temptation get the better of you.

Flaws, verses 246, 247 & 248

All created things are
impermanent.
Strive on mindfully.

Buddhacarita

Live your life in happiness, owning nothing.
Feed on happiness like lustrous gods.
Be happiness itself.

Happiness, verse 200

Desire overwhelms those who only
have pleasure as their aim in life,
whereas desire has no place in the
life of one who is self-disciplined.
Be like the mountain in the face
of a strong wind, firm and steady.

The Opposites, verses 7 & 8

It is better to conquer yourself
than to conquer thousands of others.
Victory over others is a hollow gain,
while victory over oneself is something
not even the gods can reverse.

The Thousands, verses 103, 104 & 105

Desires create suffering whether
they make you happy or sad.
Use your practice to go beyond them.

Pleasure, verse 210

Who ranks as the Highest?
One who seeks nothing.
One who is as pure
as the full moon.

The Highest, verse 413

First, look after yourself
and your practice, and then,
when you are sure of what to do,
concentrate fully on that.

Self, verse 166

Persevere with that which is enduring
and attain Nirvana.
Do not speak ill of or harm another person,
for that is not acceptable on a spiritual path.
These are the words of the Buddha.

The Buddha, verse 184

Courtesy is most precious.
Beauty without courtesy is
like a garden without flowers.

Buddhacarita

Your body is just a cosmetic plaything,
prone to disease, decay and death.
Perhaps it is time to see it for
what it really is.

Old Age, verse 147

Many flowers can make many garlands, and many worthy actions can bring many benefits.

Flowers, verse 53

A person who lies and a person
who denies their own actions
are partners on the road to hell.

Hell, verse 306

When the thirty-six streams of pleasure
are in full flow, they will drag you along.
Be aware of their pull.
Watch as a creeper grows and drags on you.
Make sure you cut it out by the root.

Desires, verses 339 & 340

Who ranks as the Highest?
One who sees everything and has
ceased this cycle of birth and death.

The Highest, verse 423

Live in accord with nature,
and if you are satisfied
there will be no wanting in your life.
This will bring you great joy.

Anguttara Nikaya

Eliminate every last desire,
just as every diseased tree
is removed from a forest,
and you will become enlightened.

The Right Way, verse 283

If you do good things you may not feel fine
until eventually you reap the consequences.
Then you will know only happiness.

Bad Conduct, verse 120

A true holy person will empty his
or her mind of all desire and hatred,
in order that they may attain Nirvana.

The Holy Person, verse 369

The foolish novice, even if he or she
spends a whole life with wise people,
will never see the Truth.
How can a spoon recognize a taste?
However, a wise novice will know
the Truth immediately,
even if it is only seen for a moment.

The Novice, verses 64 & 65

Health is the finest prize,
contentment the greatest wealth,
a good friend the finest companion
and Nirvana the greatest happiness.

Happiness, verse 204

Do not welcome praise, nor hide from blame.
Listen to your Truth and stay calm and clear.

The Wise Person, verses 81 & 82

Whatever is the cause of your suffering,
do not cause suffering to another.

Udanavarga

Sit alone.
Sleep alone.
Travel alone.
Do your *practice* alone.
Enjoy your seclusion without desire.

Other Things, verse 305

Silence does not make a person wise
if a proper life is not being adhered to.
Watch their action.
Are they in balance?
Are there only good deeds
and never bad ones?

A Proper Life, verses 268 & 269

Who ranks as the Highest?
One who has no desire,
hatred, conceit
or dishonesty.

The Highest, verse 407

If you cannot find a good companion
to travel with, walk alone, like an
elephant roaming the jungle.
It is better to be alone than to be with
those who will hinder your progress.

The Elephant, verses 329 & 330

Guard your senses.
Practice contentment and discipline.
Associate with like-minded people.
Be friendly and polite.
This is the way to Nirvana.

The Holy Person, verses 375 & 376

Envy, hatred and illusion are the roots of evil.
To be free of these is the root of good.

Majjhima Nikaya

Once you live your life in awareness,
you will live in true happiness.
This is what many great saints
have done in the past.

Awareness, verse 22

So now you are dead and you still have
not prepared yourself for this journey.
The time is now!
Practice, become cleansed and gain freedom
from the cycle of birth and death.

Flaws, verses 237 & 238

What is the noble truth
about the end of suffering?
Just ignore it.

Digha Nikaya

Anger corrupts, as weeds choke a field.
Be free of anger, and honor
those who are also free.

Desires, verse 357

Who ranks as the Highest?
One who does not even have
the desire to possess anything
of a heavenly nature.

The Highest, verse 417

Look at the world as a mirage,
as a bubble floating in front of you.
See it like this and death will have
no fear for you, and you will not be
attached to the world.

The World, verses 170 & 171

If you do no harm to others,
then you will find happiness.
If you do harm to others,
then you will find suffering.

Retribution, verses 131 & 132

Suffering arises because of consciousness.
Through the stilling of consciousness
suffering cannot be created.

Sutta Nipata

There will never be a person who receives only blame or only praise. But an enlightened being, endowed with the qualities of wisdom, insight and discipline, is free from blame.

Anger, verses 228, 229 & 230

If you are aggressive and carry out
aggressive acts in this life, you will be
reborn into increasingly aggressive lifetimes.

Anguttara Nikaya

The thoughtless person allows
desire to grow like a creeper.
From one birth to the next,
like a monkey in a forest
swinging from tree to tree,
it goes on.

Desires, verse 334

The mind, agitated and unpredictable, needs to fix on a target, in the same way an archer directs an arrow, straight and true.

Thoughts, verse 33

Follow the doctrine well
and you shall be forever safe.
This is a true blessing.

Mahamangala Sutta

Who ranks as the Highest?
One who has worked hard to overcome desire.
Who does not reap suffering because none is
caused. Who controls every thought,
word and deed.

The Highest, verses 390 & 391

Over time a pot will fill up
from just a dripping tap.
Similarly, over time good actions
will fill you with great happiness.

Bad Conduct, verse 122

It is better not to spend time with fools,
who will obstruct your practice.
Spending time with fellow aspirants
will only enhance your practice.

Happiness, verse 207

Everything must grow old.
Work upon your own salvation with haste.

Buddhacarita

Foolish people who know no better
will laugh at those on a spiritual path.
Take no notice, for their life is
full of suffering.

Self, verse 164

What is a *pleasant* feeling?
What is an *unpleasant* feeling?
What is the place in between these?

Majjhima Nikaya

There are those who see right as wrong and wrong as right.
These people are on the wrong path.

Hell, verse 318

As you are joyfully received home
after a long journey away,
so your good deeds will welcome you
when you make the journey from
this world to the next.

Pleasure, verses 219 & 220

A lack of *humility* is a person's undoing.
A lack of *generosity* destroys the gift.
Bad actions are without grace.
All these are caused by ignorance.
Address this and shine in purity.

Flaws, verses 242 & 243

When desire takes hold it turns
your life into one of suffering.
But if you overcome desire,
you overcome suffering.

Desires, verses 335 & 336

If you are always virtuous,
temptation will never trouble you,
and the fragrant scent of your good
deeds will even reach the gods.

Flowers, verses 56 & 57

It doesn't matter where you run and hide,
you cannot escape desires this way.

The Buddha, verses 188 & 189

Ideas appear and disappear.
To encourage proper ideas to
develop one must undertake practice.

Digha Nikaya

Don't concentrate on the wrong things,
do only the right things or else your
suffering will increase.
Those that follow their practice always
do what needs to be done, and this
will end their suffering.

Other Things, verses 292 & 293

Who ranks as the Highest?
One who has left anxiety behind
and, being firm in practice,
has acquired stillness of mind.

The Highest, verses 385 & 386

Regardless of whether enlightened beings appear in this world or not, there is one absolute truth. All things are impermanent and are subject to suffering.

Anguttara Nikaya

Old age doesn't necessarily make a
person a wise elder.
Look for truth, non-violence, restraint
and self-discipline, and then you may
call that person an elder.

A Proper Life, verses 260 & 261

If you do something bad
there is nowhere to hide.

Bad Conduct, verse 127

In ancient times elephants were used in battle
and withstood the onslaught of many arrows.
In your life, accept criticism whether it is
justified or not.

The Elephant, verse 320

Be like an island that no flood can engulf.
To become like this, meditate, exercise
self-control, persevere with your practice
and live in awareness.

Awareness, verse 25

The true aspirant is always striving
for freedom and, as they have no home,
is always moving onwards.

The Enlightened One, verse 91

Those who have not followed a spiritual path
will wither away as they get older.
All they will be able to do is look
back and reminisce about times past.

Old Age, verses 155 & 156

If you want release from suffering then
be done with doubt, desire and passion.
Strengthen your practice, understand
goodness and truth, and you
will be free of suffering.

Desires, verses 349 & 350

If you adhere to
what is taught by
your teacher, your
life will be full of
happiness.

The Wise Person, verse 79

The best time to learn the discipline of practice is when you are young and strong. It is too late otherwise.

The Right Way, verse 280

Who ranks as the Highest?
One who watches things die
and then be reborn,
and is not attached to this cycle.
One who lives a proper life.

The Highest, verse 419

Be restrained in your actions,
and live the four noble truths.
This will lead you to Nirvana.
This is a true blessing.

Mahamangala Sutta

It is no good reciting the scriptures
if you don't live your life by them.
It is better to know a few texts well, to
overcome desire and live your life properly.
This will give you a wonderful life.

The Opposites, verses 19 & 20

Live in accord with nature,
and if you are detached
there will be no wanting in your life.
This will give you liberation.

Anguttara Nikaya

Pull yourself together and focus on your practice.
Make sure you stay on the right path and
your life will be one of happiness.

The World, verses 168 & 169

The novice who knows he or she is just that,
has a small amount of wisdom.
But the novice who thinks he or she is wise,
is a fool.

The Novice, verse 63

There is no fire like passion,
no scourge like hatred, no ache like hunger,
no suffering greater than mental anguish,
no happiness greater than peace,
and nothing greater than Nirvana.

Happiness, verses 202 & 203

Does it really matter whether
someone else is innocent or guilty?
Only worry about yourself
and your own actions.

Amagandha Sutta

As certainly as a drover leads
cows to new pasture,
so old age and death are inevitable.

Retribution, verse 135

Effort given to satisfying material
desires is rewarded only with
suffering and fear.
Avoid material desires and
you avoid suffering and fear.

Pleasure, verse 212

Half-hearted attempts at your practice will allow delusion to continue entering your life. Only complete focus will stop delusion from entering, and destroy old patterns.

Majjhima Nikaya

What do you think is better:
to seek for a partner,
or to seek for the Self?

Buddhacarita

Live one meditative day well, with
freedom, strength and wisdom,
rather than a hundred years
in laziness and bondage.

The Thousands, verses 112 & 113

Speak the truth,
don't give in to anger,
and be generous.
Follow these three principles
and be wise.

Anger, verse 224

The true holy person has a mind so still that
the most wonderful peace can be experienced.
As mundane existence is considered, the joy of
truth wells up in the heart of one so practised.

The Holy Person, verses 373 & 374

In the noble eightfold path,
what is Right Intention?
The intention to be free from desire.
The intention not to harm or be cruel.

Digha Nikaya

Who ranks as the Highest?
One who has no thought of good and bad.
One who has great strength and courage.

The Highest, verse 418

To try and follow those who have no home,
no possessions, who control their senses
and consumption of food, is like trying to
follow a flock of birds flying through the air.

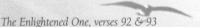

The Enlightened One, verses 92 & 93

Keep your mind fixed on non-violence and be sure in meditation both day and night.

Other Things, verses 300 & 301

If you over-eat, over-sleep and
become too lazy to do anything,
then rebirth is certain,
time and time again.

The Elephant, verse 325

There is a time for the
Truth to be revealed to you.
If you don't believe it
then it is your loss.

Buddhacarita

Bad actions committed by a person will eventually return to cause them suffering.

Self, verse 161

It is good indeed to honor all Buddhas
and their disciples, to follow one's practice
and to live in harmony with other aspirants.
This will give you great merit
as you journey onwards.

The Buddha, verses 194, 195 & 196

When the time comes for
death to seek you out,
there is nowhere to hide.

Bad Conduct, verse 128

Be forever cautious among the worldly,
alert among the apathetic.
With this attitude you will soon leave others
behind, since this will mark you as aware,
while others will be seen as idle.

Awareness, verses 29 & 30

The mind, frightened by the lure
of desire exerted by the material world,
will thrash about like a fish freshly caught.

Thoughts, verse 34

In the same way that a florist chooses the right flowers for a garland, so you must make the right choice for your own spiritual path, in order that you may go beyond this world – beyond the world of death and beyond the world of the gods.

Flowers, verses 44 & 45

Everyone wants to enjoy life to the full,
but material pleasure will tie you to
a life of birth and death.
Running here and there, from one
pleasure to the next, is not going
to release you from suffering.

Desires, verses 341, 342 & 343

When you become enlightened,
when your good deeds overcome bad,
you will illuminate the world as the moon
does when it breaks free from the clouds.

The World, verses 172 & 173

Rise above the five obstacles and
be free of the five attachments.
This will lead you to the greatest happiness.

The Holy Person, verse 370

You are like a withered leaf,
ready to crumble in death's hand,
and what preparations have you made?
The time is now!
Practice, become cleansed and be ready.

Flaws, verses 235 & 236

Live in accord with nature,
and if you see things as they really are
there will be no wanting in your life.
This will give you detachment.

Anguttara Nikaya

You are what you think.
Pain will follow bad thoughts
as certain as happiness
will follow good ones.

The Opposites, verses 1 & 2

Just because a person begs for their daily needs,
it does not mean they are living a proper life.
Look for chastity, non-attachment and
discipline in practice before you award
such an accolade.

A Proper Life, verses 266 & 267

If someone decries your faith, your belief,
don't allow anger to take control.

Brahmajala Sutta

In the same way the moon follows
a set path between the stars,
keep yourself fixed in the presence
of a wise teacher and fellow aspirants.

Happiness, verse 208

The novice will only realize suffering
when the fruits of his or her bad deed are born.
Until then everything will be sweet as honey.
Even though they may fast assiduously,
it means nothing if they don't understand truth.

The Novice, verses 69 & 70

What leads to the end of suffering?
The noble eightfold path.

Digha Nikaya

Speak gently to everyone and they will respond accordingly. Harsh words hurt, and you will get them thrown back in your face.

Retribution, verse 133

If you have the good fortune
to find a wise teacher, then follow
him or her and let them reveal
hidden spiritual treasures.
You can only benefit from this.

The Wise Person, verse 76

One thing is certain: your body will get old, decay and die.

Old Age, verse 148

Speak little, speak only good and do not judge.
Be moderate in food consumption and sleep.
Follow your practice.
These are the words of the Buddha.

The Buddha, verse 185

As a blade of grass can cut your finger,
so an improper life by a so-called renunciant
will only cause greater suffering.

Hell, verse 311

There are six types of perception:
form, sound, smell, taste, touch and ideas.
But what does one perceive?

Anguttara Nikaya

It is hard to live in the world
and hard to live outside it.
It is difficult to live with those who
revel in the world and difficult not
to have a permanent home.
Be at peace and your suffering will end.

Other Things, verse 302

If there is no open wound on your hand,
then no infection can harm you.
Similarly, no harm will come to you
if you undertake no harmful actions.

Bad Conduct, verse 124

Dig up and destroy the root of desire if you do not want temptation to control your life. For a tree which has been cut down will grow again if given the chance, and so will desire if the roots are not destroyed.

Desires, verses 337 & 338

It is not how you look to the world
that matters, but how you act.
Observe your practice and
rid yourself of desire.
You will then become the Highest.

The Highest, verses 395 & 396

Birth, old age and death are all suffering.
Grief, regret, discomfort, sadness
and despair are all suffering.
The five factors of attachment are suffering.

Digha Nikaya

Death carries away people engrossed in sensual pleasures, in the same way that a flood will sweep away a sleeping village.

Flowers, verses 47 & 48

As a plant sheds its withered flowers,
so you must shed your desires and hatred.
Be at peace in thought, word and deed,
and let go of all attachment.
This is the way of a true holy person.

The Holy Person, verses 377 & 378

Live in accord with nature,
and if you are happy
there will be no wanting in your life.
This will give you concentration.

Anguttara Nikaya

Who ranks as the Highest?
One who is wise, heroic,
courageous and strong.

The Highest, verse 422

Don't have preferences,
don't become attached.
If you have no likes and dislikes,
no attachments, you will be free.

Pleasure, verse 211

One well-chosen word or one well-chosen
line of poetry, which brings the listener peace,
is better than a thousand spoken in vain.
One verse of the Buddha's teaching,
which is certain to bring the listener peace,
is better than a thousand spoken for no reason.

The Thousands, verses 100, 101 & 102

Everything is illusion.
Learn this and you will be free
from suffering.

The Right Way, verse 279

Be gentle and patient.
Gather together with other
peaceful people and speak
gently of spiritual subjects.
This is a true blessing.

Mahamangala Sutta

Awareness is lost on those who
are not on a spiritual path.
For those who are spiritual seekers
it is the greatest gift.

Awareness, verse 26

It is up to you whether you do
bad things or hurt someone.
Do not do either.
We all have the choice to be good or bad,
no one makes that choice for us.

Self, verse 165

To have good friends is truly excellent.
To have good friends when you die is
absolutely wonderful.
But best of all it is good to overcome suffering.

The Elephant, verse 331

Whatever befalls you, even if it be death, do not let dark thoughts enter your mind. Make a great effort to establish mindfulness and calm the body and mind so that both are firm and resolved.

Majjhima Nikaya

If your teacher disciplines you,
instructs you on what is right,
or restrains you from doing wrong,
such a person will be loved by the good
and reviled by the bad.

The Wise Person, verse 77

Learn that nothing is real
and that all living things suffer,
and you will be free from suffering.
This is the path to enlightenment.

The Right Way, verses 277 & 278

Be *gentle* and abolish anger.
Be *good* and overcome bad.
Be *generous* and conquer greed.
Be *truthful* and extinguish deception.

Anger, verse 223

There is a place where there is neither
earth, nor air, nor fire, nor water, where
there is no consciousness, nor space,
nor void, nor perception. There is neither
a coming nor a going, neither a standing
still, nor a falling away, without being
fixed, nor without moving, without basis.
It is the end of suffering.

Buddhacarita

If you find yourself with no support on the spiritual path, then walk on alone. There is no point in trying to learn from those who have nothing to teach.

The Novice, verse 61

Selfishness corrupts,
as weeds choke a field.
Be free of selfishness,
and honor those
who are also free.

Desires, verse 359

Be careful what you do
and try not to drink alcohol.
Never tire of helping others.
This is a true blessing.

Mahamangala Sutta

A true holy person speaks little,
but when necessary uses words
which are sweet.
You will always see them following
their practice, rejoicing in truth
and being constant in truth.

The Holy Person, verses 363 & 364

An untrained mind is your greatest enemy,
while a disciplined mind is your greatest friend.

Thoughts, verses 42 & 43

Avoid bad actions, just as a merchant travelling alone avoids dangerous roads, and a lover of life avoids poison.

Bad Conduct, verse 123

There is no stairway to the sky,
no hiding place for fools and their desires.
Others seem to revel in their misery,
while you can transcend suffering,
unshaken by change,
steady in practice and freedom.

Flaws, verses 254 & 255

Live in accord with nature,
and when you are relaxed there
will be no wanting in your life.
You will know great happiness.

Anguttara Nikaya

A disciplined horse needs no whip,
and neither does the disciplined mind.
Both are trained in good habits
as a way of life.

Retribution, verses 143 & 144

Who ranks as the Highest?
One who does not live in the past,
the present or the future.

The Highest, verse 420

The fragrance of virtue stands alone,
without equal.

Flowers, verse 55

Swans fly along the path of the sun,
and psychics seem to move beyond the world.
Forget them; you must concentrate on your
practice and attain Nirvana.

The World, verse 175

How can you enjoy material things,
sensual pleasures, when the world
is tumbling down around your ears?
Stop living in darkness and search
for the light.

Old Age, verse 146

An enlightened being is much sought
after by everyone, even the gods.

The Buddha, verse 181

There are those who are sorry for deeds
which they need not worry about,
and not sorry for deeds which they
should worry about.
These people are on the wrong path.

Hell, verse 316

Once you reach the end
of your spiritual journey,
you will find freedom,
a release from suffering.

The Enlightened One, verse 90

In the noble eightfold path,
what is Right Understanding?
Knowledge about suffering and
from where suffering came.
Knowledge about the end of suffering,
and how to reach the end of suffering.

Digha Nikaya

The correct way of living is not found
simply by discussing the theory of it.
Even without study you can experience it,
but you have to live it.

A Proper Life, verse 259

The mind that stays focused
when everything around it is crazy,
giving in neither to passion
nor sadness;
this is a true blessing.

Mahamangala Sutta

If you look like a recluse, it doesn't make you one.
It is by your actions that you are judged.
There is no point in taking the role of a recluse
or an initiate if your mind is full of desire.

The Highest, verses 393 & 394

People think highly of someone following a spiritual path, who is committed to their practice and living their life properly.

Pleasure, verse 217

Keep your mind fixed on holy company and be aware of the nature of your physical body both day and night.

Other Things, verses 298 & 299

If you dwell on bad thoughts then
your life will be full of negativity.
However, if you don't allow bad thoughts
you will be free of all things negative.

The Opposites, verses 3 & 4

Once you have your own
self in order, then you can
help others to do the same.

Self, verse 158

Who ranks as the Highest?
One who does not crave pleasure.
For this is the end of suffering.

The Highest, verses 401 & 402

You will be rewarded with four gifts
if all you do is honor an enlightened being;
they are health, happiness, beauty and longevity.
This honoring is far more worthy than
making shallow gifts and offerings.

The Thousands, verses 108 & 109

Do you speak of that which
you know yourself, is seen
by yourself and is found by yourself?

Buddhacarita

The good desire nothing, do not speak of cravings and, regardless of what happens, are not influenced by good or bad. Such actions will highlight them as special people.

The Wise Person, verses 83 & 84

Release the past, the present and the future.
Give your mind the freedom it needs to
take you beyond suffering.

Desires, verse 348

Once your mind is still, and your words and actions peaceful, you will be free from delusion and opposites, and ready for the final step to enlightenment.

The Enlightened One, verses 96 & 97

In the noble eightfold path,
what is Right Speech?
Not to indulge in lies, gossip,
or other thoughtless speech.

Digha Nikaya

Give up anger and pride
and have no attachments.
If you do not possess anybody
or anything, you will not have
to endure suffering.

Anger, verse 221

Foolish novices are their own worst enemies, sowing bad deeds and reaping the consequences almost immediately, which you can see by the amount of suffering they are going through.

The Novice, verses 66 & 67

A monarch's carriage eventually loses its shine and, similarly, the body decays. Enlightened beings have told us that truth and goodness live on.

Old Age, verse 151

Keep trying and you shall be free
of sensuality and ignorance.

Buddhacarita

For a person without conscience,
life seems easy.
For a person striving to be pure,
the journey is hard.

Flaws, verses 244 & 245

Live in accord with nature
and follow a proper life,
and you will want for nothing.

Anguttara Nikaya

Follow the Buddha, follow your practice
and follow fellow aspirants; learn the four noble
truths and then enter the noble eightfold path,
and only then can you be free from suffering.

The Buddha, verses 190, 191 & 192

Once you are living your life in awareness,
it will be as though you stand high
above others, witnessing their suffering,
while you do not suffer at all.

Awareness, verse 28

Without realizing, it is easy
to carry out bad deeds.
However, retribution will come,
as certain as you would burn your
hand if you placed it too close to a fire.

Retribution, verse 136

If you find a good companion,
who is following the same spiritual path,
travel together, overcoming obstacles
as they arise.

The Elephant, verse 328

Avoid extremes in life.
The middle way gives sight to
the eyes and clarity to the mind,
and this leads to wisdom, to peace,
and onward to Nirvana.

Buddhacarita

Over time a pot will fill up
from just a dripping tap.
Similarly, over time bad actions
will fill you with great suffering.

Bad Conduct, verse 121

Who ranks as the Highest?
One who is a wanderer without desire.

The Highest, verse 416

The eightfold path is the best to follow.
The four noble truths the best to adhere to.
Non-attachment the best frame of mind.
An enlightened being the best of humans.

The Right Way, verse 273

Do not serve the foolish,
but look after the wise.
Honor those worthy of honor.
This is a true blessing.

Mahamangala Sutta

There is no justification for
harming any living thing.
If you do not hurt anything or anyone,
you will be held in high esteem.

A Proper Life, verse 270

A true holy person has control
over all things and uses action
to serve others.
With meditation central to their
being, their life is free of suffering.

The Holy Person, verse 362

Live your life in happiness,
even though those around you
lead lives which are unhealthy,
and wish to spread their illness to you.
Be happiness itself.

Happiness, verse 198

Few people see the light of truth
within this world of darkness,
in the same way few birds escape
from the net which has caught them.

The World, verse 174

There are those who see wrong
where there is wrong and right
where there is right.
They are following the right path
to the greatest happiness.

Hell, verse 319

Effort given to satisfying idle fancies
is rewarded only with sadness and fear.
Avoid idle fancies and you avoid sadness
and fear.

Pleasure, verse 214

A true Buddhist stands out
among ordinary people,
just as the lotus flower grows
tall among weeds.

Flowers, verses 58 & 59

In the noble eightfold path,
what is Right Action?
Not to kill, not to steal and
not to engage in sexual misconduct.

Digha Nikaya

The Buddhist Year

There are many celebration days in the Buddhist world, and invariably these are days of great merriment. They will be full of offerings, food distribution, and talks of Buddhist teaching, concluding with chanting and meditation. Presented here is a selected list, although I would like to point out that with the general exception of the Buddha's birthday, many of the festivals and holy days can be specific to a country, region and/or Buddhist tradition. Another point to bear in mind is that most of the festivals are based around the lunar calendar, and will therefore change on a yearly basis. With that said, I hope the following list is useful.

VESAK/VISAKAH PUJA Buddha's Birthday

In most circles, the Buddha's birthday is known as Vesak or Visakah. However, it celebrates not only the Buddha's birthday, but also his enlightenment and death. This day falls on the first Full Moon day in May, except in leap years when it moves to June.

THE BUDDHIST NEW YEAR

In countries which practice Theravada, the new year starts on the first Full Moon in April (it may be celebrated for three days). In those countries where Mahayana is practiced it starts on the first Full Moon in January. However, this varies widely and can fall any time between January and April.

MAGHA PUJA DAY Sangha Day

This festival takes place on the day of the Full Moon in the third lunar month and commemorates a gathering (sangha) held by the Buddha in Sarnath, which is just north of Varanasi. At this time, 1,250 enlightened saints returned to the Buddha of their own accord (1), without prior arrangement (2), to the one who taught them (3) on Full Moon day (4). For these four reasons it is also called the Fourfold Assembly.

ASALHA PUJA DAY Dhamma Day

To commemorate the Buddha's first teaching — the turning of the wheel of Dhamma — this day is celebrated on the Full Moon of the eighth lunar month.

UPOSATHA Observance Day

In Theravada countries there are four monthly holy days which continue to be observed. These days are the New Moon, Full Moon and first and last Quarter Moon days. This is also known in Sri Lanka as Poya Day.

THE PLOUGHING FESTIVAL

Known in Thailand as Raek Na, *this festival is celebrated in May when the moon is half full. It celebrates the Buddha's first moment of enlightenment when, at the age of seven, he joined his father to watch a field being ploughed.*

Further Reading

The Dhammapada exists in many versions, each slightly different. Choose one that appeals to you from your local bookstore. To find out more about Buddhism, the following list provides a good starting point.

Batchelor, Stephen, *The Awakening of the West*. Albany, CA: Parallax Press, 1994

Boorstein, Silvia, *It's Easier Than You Think*. Harper San Francisco, 1997

Boucher, Sandy, *Opening the Lotus*. NY: Ballantine Books, 1998

Chodron, Pema, *When Things Fall Apart*. Boston: Shambhala, 1997

The Dalai Lama, *Freedom in Exile*. Harper San Francisco, 1998

Hagen, Steve, *Buddhism Plain and Simple*. Boston: Charles E. Tuttle, 1997

Harvey, Peter, *An Introduction to Buddhism*. Cambridge University Press, 1990

Kiew Kit, Wong, *The Complete Book of Zen*. Boston: Tuttle Publishing, 2002

Kornfield, Jack, *A Path with Heart*. NY: Bantam Doubleday Dell Publications, 1993

Low, Albert, *An Invitation to Practice Zen*. Boston: Charles E. Tuttle, 1989

O'Halloran, Maura, *Pure Heart, Enlightened Mind*. Boston: Charles E. Tuttle, 1994

Okumura, Shohaku and Dan Leighton, *The Wholehearted Way: A Translation of Eihei Dogen's Bendowa*. Boston: Charles E. Tuttle, 1997

Senzaki, Nyogen and Paul Reps, *Zen Flesh, Zen Bones*. Boston: Charles E. Tuttle, 1998

Trungpa, Chögyam, *The Heart of the Buddha*. Boston: Shambhala, 1991

Useful periodicals include *Tricycle* and *Shambala Sun*.

Useful Addresses

For a complete guide to centers in your area, refer to *The Buddhist Directory* compiled by Peter Lorie and Julie Foakes (Charles E. Tuttle, 1997).

BUDDHIST ASSOCIATION OF USA
3070 Albany Crescent
Bronx, NY 10472
Tel: (718) 884 9111

FRIENDS OF THE WESTERN BUDDHIST ORDER
Arya Loka Retreat Center
Hartwood Circle
Newmarket, NH 03857
Tel: (603) 659 5456

RIGPA FELLOWSHIP
449 Powell Street
Suite 200
San Francisco, CA 94102
Tel: (415) 392 2055

Author's acknowledgements

I would like to thank Tessa Strickland for her help with this project, which has gone far beyond that of a conventional agent/client relationship, and also Dr Stuart Rose for his invaluable assistance. I must mention the excellent people at Eddison Sadd who have worked very hard with what seems like never-ending enthusiasm on producing the finished article. Of course, the inspiration and guidance has come from my beloved teacher Sri Sathya Sai Baba, without whom my life would still be an empty shell.

Please Note

Although every effort has been made to credit text sources, this book may lack some references. Any authors, or their representatives, will happily be credited as soon as they are heard from or located.